Collins

easy learning

Spelling

Ages 5–6

pear

pair

Karina Law

How to use this book

- Find a quiet, comfortable place to work, away from distractions.
- Tackle one topic at a time.
- Help with reading the instructions where necessary and ensure that your child understands what to do.
- Encourage your child to check their own answers as they complete each activity.
- Discuss with your child what they have learnt.
- Let your child return to their favourite pages once they have been completed, to talk about the activities.
- Reward your child with plenty of praise and encouragement.

Special features

- Yellow boxes: Introduce a topic and outline the key spelling ideas.
- Suggests when your child can use a dictionary to help with the spelling or understanding of a word.
- Orange shaded boxes: Suggest activities and encourage discussion with your child about what they have learnt.

Learning a new word

When your child is learning a new word, use the 'Look and say, cover, write, check' method.

- Look at the word and say it aloud.
- Cover it.
- Write it.
- Check it.

You could also try the following ideas:

- Break the word up into smaller parts, for example, cup-board.
- Pronounce the word exactly as it is written, for example, Wed-nes-day.
- Break the word up into separate phonemes (sounds), for example, sh-ee-p.

Published by Collins
An imprint of HarperCollinsPublishers
1 London Bridge Street
London SE1 9GF

Browse the complete Collins catalogue at
www.collins.co.uk

© HarperCollinsPublishers Limited 2006
This edition © HarperCollinsPublishers 2015

10 9

ISBN 978-0-00-813436-5

Printed in Great Britain by Martins the Printers

The author asserts the moral right to be identified as the author of this work.

The author and publisher are grateful to the copyright holders for permission to use the quoted materials and images.

Images are © HarperCollinsPublishers and © Shutterstock.com

Written by Karina Law
Design and layout by Graham M Brasnett and Contentra Technologies
Illustrated by Andy Tudor
Cover design by Sarah Duxbury and Paul Oates
Project managed by Sonia Dawkins

Contents

How to use this book — 2

Short vowels — 4

Syllables — 5

Long vowels with e — 6

Spelling patterns: sh, ch, th — 8

Spelling pattern: tch — 9

Word ending: ck — 10

Spelling patterns: k, nk — 11

Word endings: ff, ll, ss, zz — 12

More than one — 13

Vowel sound: ee, ea, ie, y — 14

Vowel sound: ai, ay — 15

Vowel sound: ie, y, igh — 16

Vowel sound: oa, ow, oe — 17

Vowel sound: oo, ew, ue — 18

Spelling pattern: ar — 19

Spelling patterns: ow, ou — 20

Spelling patterns: air, are, ear, ere — 21

Spelling patterns: or, oor, aw, au, ore — 22

Spelling patterns: er, ir, ur — 23

Spelling patterns: wh, ph — 24

Word endings: ing, ed, er — 25

Spelling patterns: ear, ea — 26

Compound words — 27

Prefix: un — 28

Adding er and est — 29

Spelling tips — 30

Answers — 32

Short vowels

There are five vowels.

a e i o u

Most words in the English language contain at least one vowel.

1 Write the missing vowel in each word.

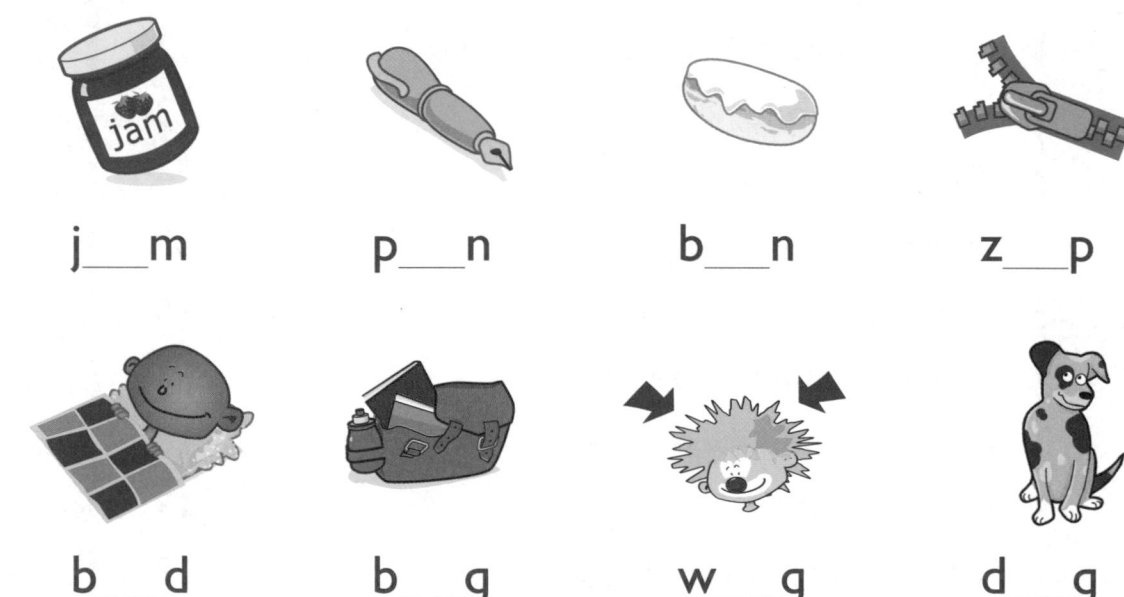

j__m   p__n   b__n   z__p

b__d   b__g   w__g   d__g

2 Change the vowel in each word to make a new word.

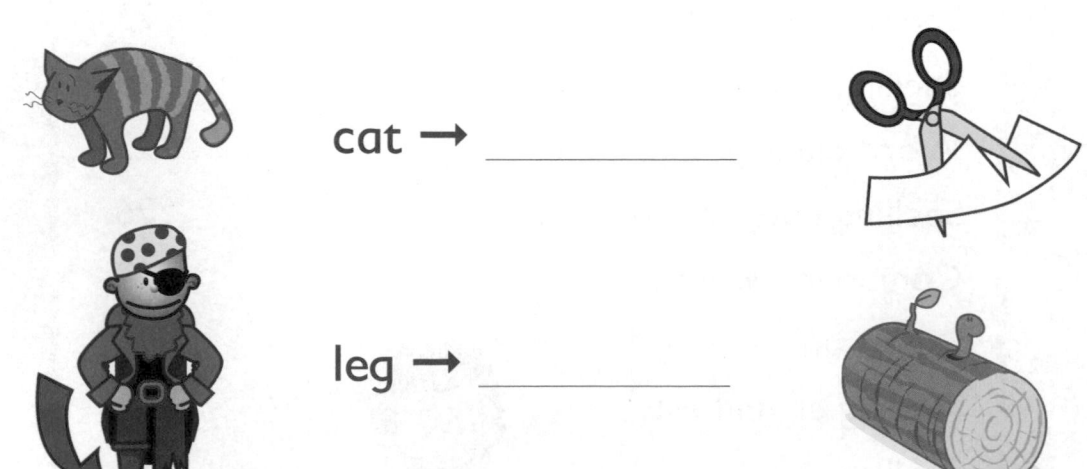

cat → _____

leg → _____

Syllables

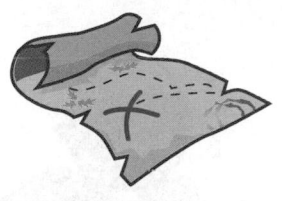

map

has 1 syllable.

donkey

has 2 syllables.

crocodile

has 3 syllables.

Every syllable has a vowel sound.

1 Say each word aloud. How many syllables do you hear?

Colour 1 star for 1 syllable. Colour 2 stars for 2 syllables.
Colour 3 stars for 3 syllables.

Knowing that there is a vowel sound in every syllable helps with spelling. Make sure your child can hear each syllable as you say a word aloud. Clapping can help children to count individual syllables in words.

Long vowels with e

Say the word. Add the letter **e**. Say the new word.
Can you hear a change in the vowel sound?

 cap + e → cape

The vowel in c**a**p is a **short vowel**.
When we add **e** to this word, the first vowel becomes a **long vowel**.

1 Add **e** to the end of each word to make a new word.

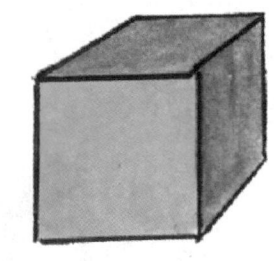

cub → cub____

not → not____

kit → kit____

plan → plan____

Long vowels sound the same as their letter names.

2 Write words that rhyme.

 + **ake**

cake _____

_____ _____

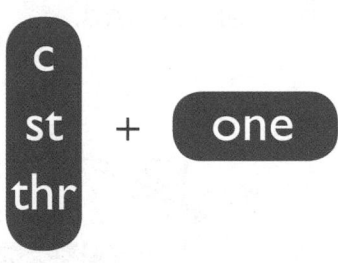 + **one**

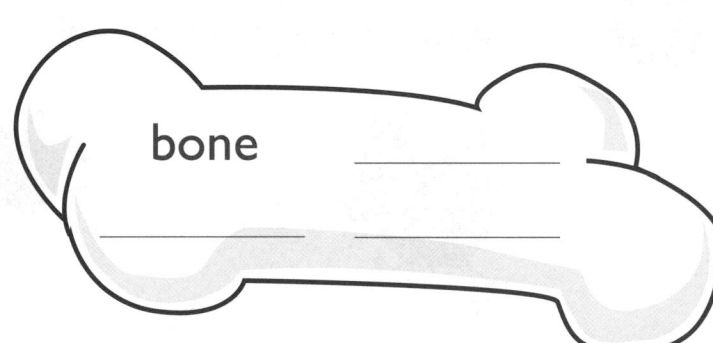

bone _____

_____

3 Change one letter to make a new word.

race ➔ ___ace

bake ➔ b___ke

nose ➔ ___ose

fire ➔ fi___e  **5**

mile ➔ m___le

mice ➔ ___ice

Spelling patterns: sh, ch, th

Listen to **sh**, **ch** and **th** in these words.

sheep

cheese

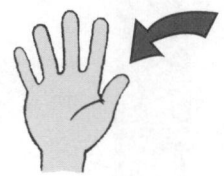

thumb

1 Join **sh** and **ch** to the things that start with their sound.

sh   **ch**

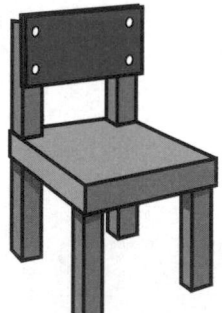

What does a sea monster eat for lunch?

Fish and **ships**!

2 Write **sh**, **ch** or **th** at the end of each word.

fi____   bea____   too____   bru____

ru____   mo____   fini____   lun____

Spelling pattern: tch

The **ch** sound is usually spelt as **tch** when it comes after a single vowel.

1 Add a vowel to each of these **tch** words.

| vowels: a e i o u |

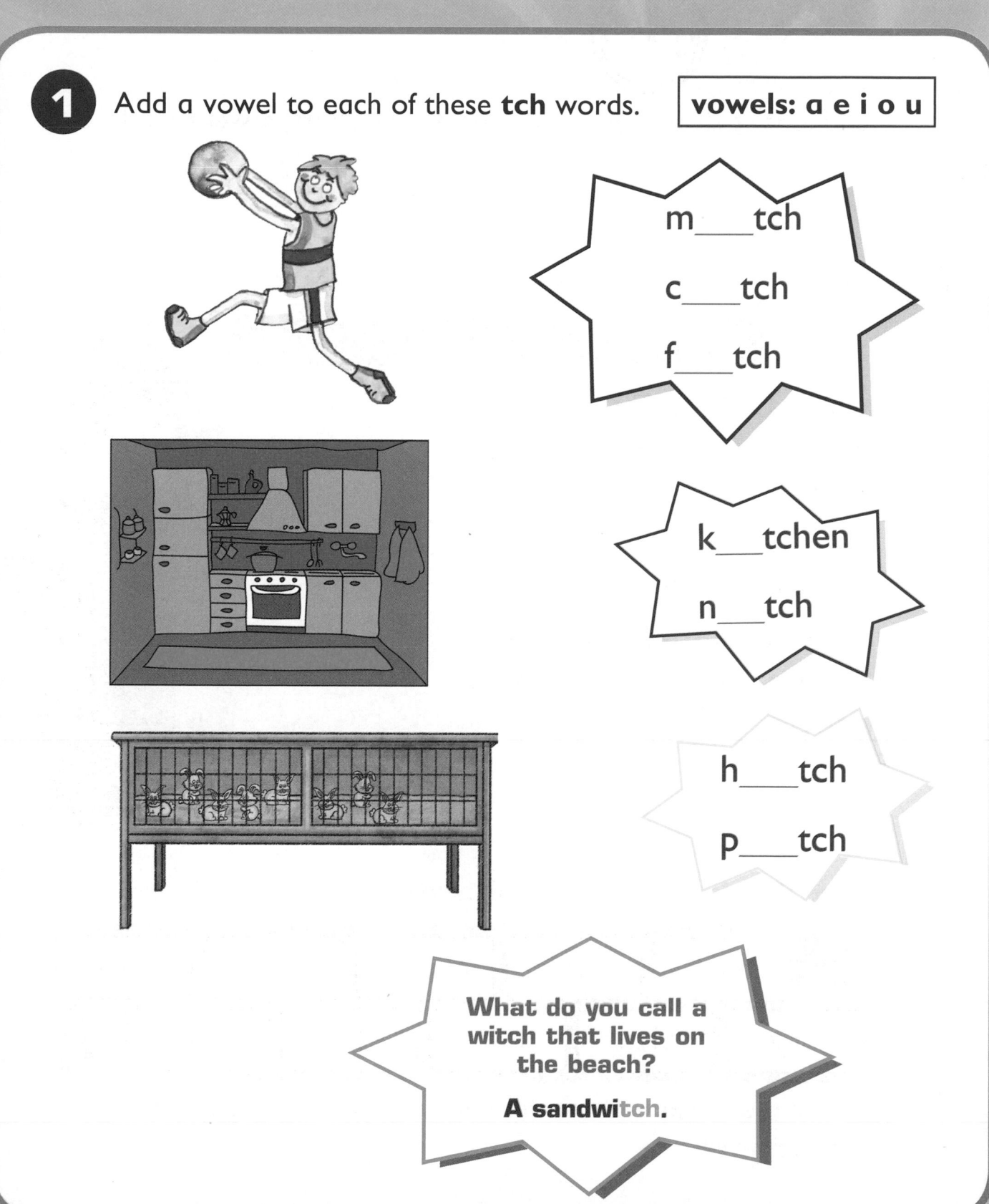

m___tch

c___tch

f___tch

k___tchen

n___tch

h___tch

p___tch

What do you call a
witch that lives on
the beach?

A sandwitch.

Word ending: ck

Listen to the sound of **ck** at the end of clo**ck**.

The 'k' sound is spelt **ck** when it comes after a short vowel sound.

1 Complete the rhymes. Choose a **ck** word to write in each space.

> sock   clock   stuck   struck

Hickory Dickory Dock,
A mouse ran up the _____.
The clock _____ one,
The mouse ran down,
Hickory Dickory Dock.

Hickory Dickory Dock,
A mouse chewed a hole in my _____.
My toe _____ out,
The mouse ran about,
Hickory Dickory Dock.

2 Read the **ck** words in the wall below.

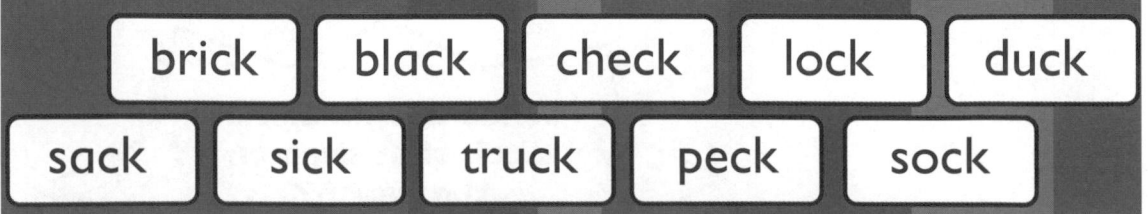

| brick | black | check | lock | duck |
| sack | sick | truck | peck | sock |

Colour the bricks. Use a different colour for each pair of rhyming words.

Spelling patterns: k, nk

The 'k' sound is spelt **k** rather than **c** when it comes before **e**, **i** and **y**.

kettle

kitten

spooky

1 Write **e**, **i** or **y** in each word.

spook_   k_d   k_tchup

k_nnel   k_ng   risk_

Listen to the sound of **nk** in drink.

2 Read aloud the **nk** words. Colour all the words that rhyme with **pink**.

bank   think   junk   link   tank

stink   shrink   blink   trunk

Now write the words that **don't** rhyme with pink.

_____ _____

_____ _____

Word endings: ff, ll, ss, zz

gruff   well   princess   buzz

The double consonant in each word makes a single sound.

1   Write **ff**, **ll** or **ss** in each space.

Jack and Ji____ went up the hi ____.

The prince____ gave the

frog a ki____.

I'll hu____ and I'll pu____ and

I'll blow your house down!

The 'f', 'l', 's' and 'z' sounds are usually spelt as ff, ll, ss and zz if they come straight after a single vowel letter in short words.

More than one

We usually add **s** to the end of a word when there is more than one of something.

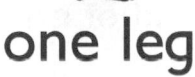 one leg  lots of legs

For a word that ends in **s**, **x**, **sh** or **ch**, we usually add **es**.

 buses    foxes   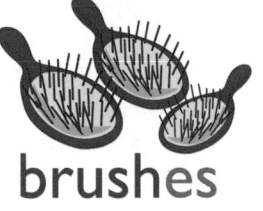 brushes    peaches

1 Add **s** or **es** to the end of each word.

a pair of sock____

a bunch of banana____

some sweet____

dish____

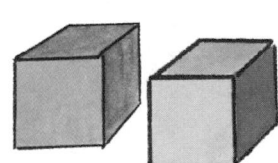

box____

monster____

sandwich____

spider____

octopus____

Vowel sound: ee, ea, ie, y

Listen to the sound of **ee** in b**ee**.

Listen to the same sound of **ea** in b**ea**d.

Listen to the same sound of **ie** in th**ie**f.

1 Think of three more words with **ee**. Write them on the beehive.

bee

2 Read these words aloud. Colour the odd one out in each row.

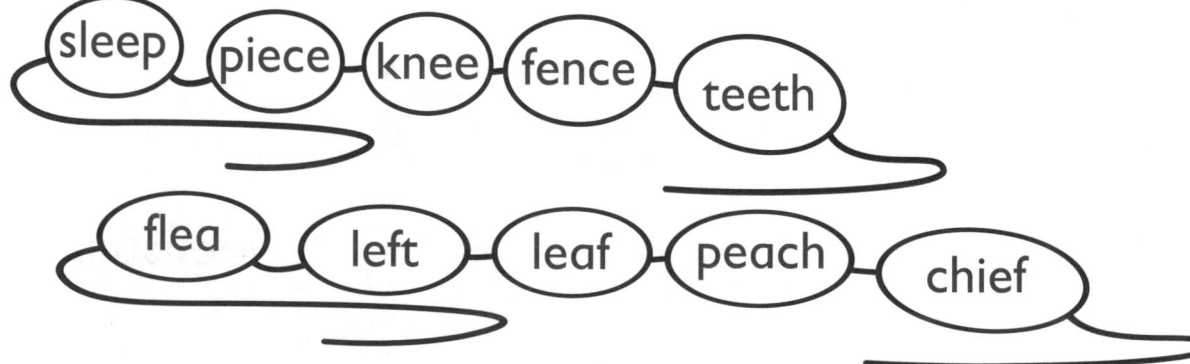

sleep   piece   knee   fence   teeth

flea   left   leaf   peach   chief

3 The letter **y** at the end of a word often makes an **ee** sound.
Add **y** to each word. Read aloud the words you have made.

ver____   happ____   sill____   funn____   sorr____

part____   sunn____   famil____   laz____   twent____

Vowel sound: ai, ay

Listen to the sound of **ai** in sn**ai**l.

The **ai** sound is usually spelt **ay** at the end of words.

Listen to the same sound of **ay** in pl**ay**.

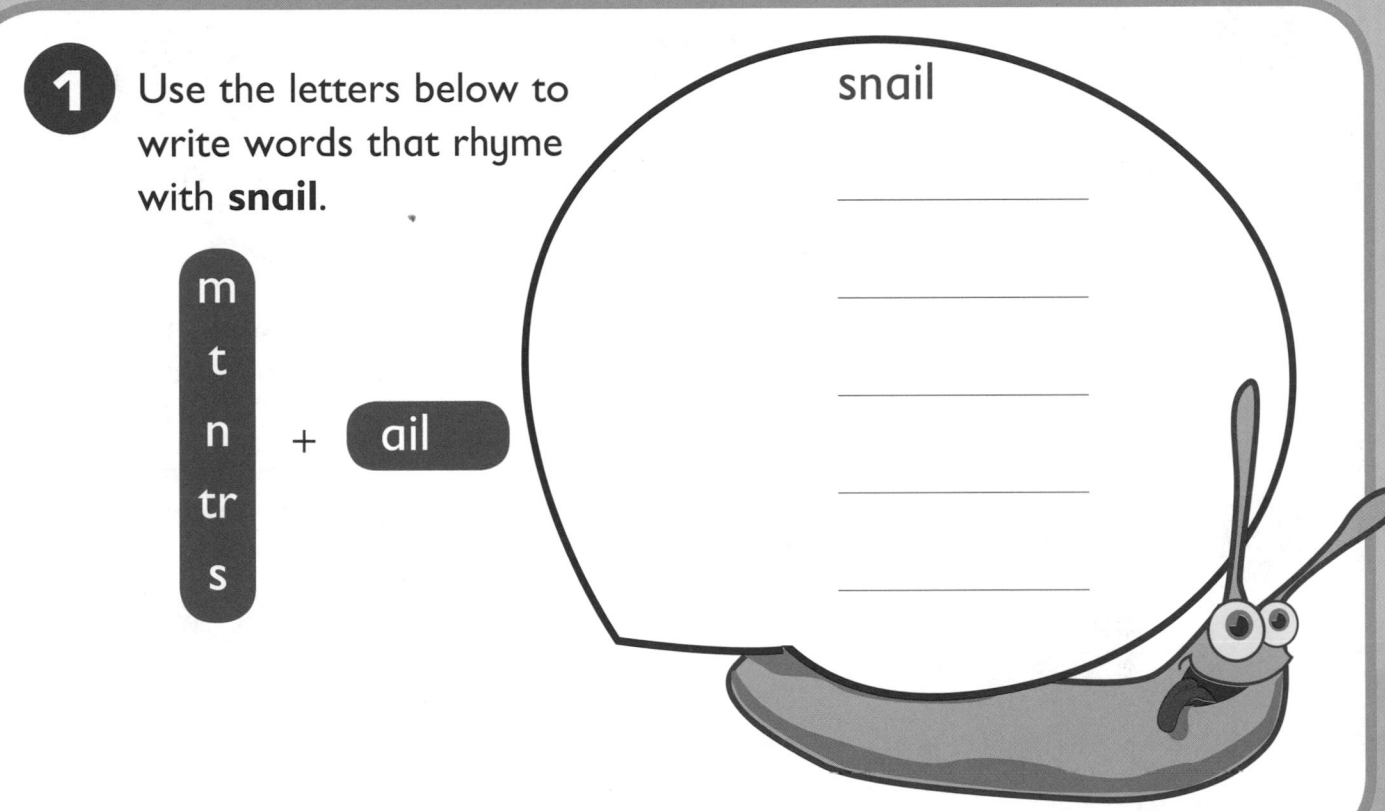

1 Use the letters below to write words that rhyme with **snail**.

m
t
n
tr
s

+ ail

snail

_____

_____

_____

_____

_____

2 Write **ai** or **ay** in these words. Remember that **ay** is usually used at the end of words.

tr____   tr____n   tod____

aw____   afr____d   s____

cl____   st____   p____nt

Vowel sound: ie, y, igh

Listen to the sound of **ie** in p**ie**.

Listen to the sound of **y** in fl**y**.

Listen to the same sound of **igh** in h**igh**.

1 Write rhyming words with **y** or **ie**.

fly	cr____	t____	fly
fr____	p____	sp____	
tr____	wh____	l____	

What is the difference between a bird and a fly?

A bird can fly **but a f**ly **can't bird!**

2 Write words that rhyme with **knight**.

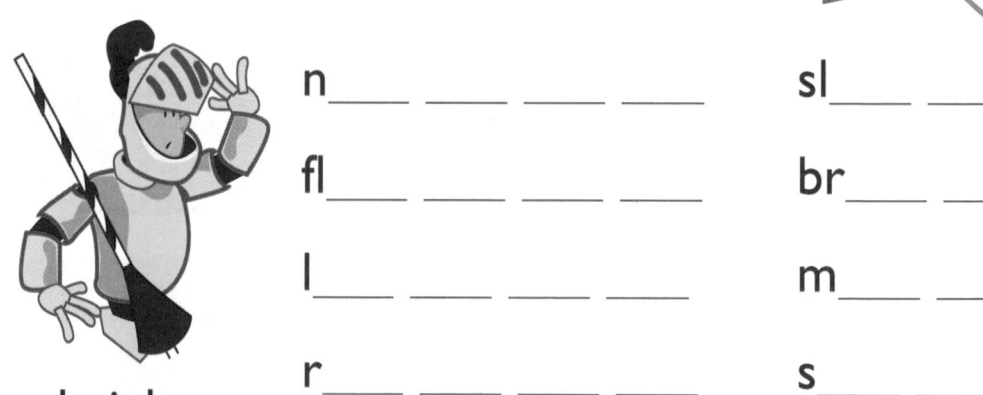

n____ ____ ____ ____   sl____ ____ ____ ____

fl____ ____ ____ ____   br____ ____ ____ ____

l____ ____ ____ ____   m____ ____ ____ ____

r____ ____ ____ ____   s____ ____ ____ ____

knight

3 Finish the sentences. Write a word with **igh** in each space.

My shoes are too t____ ____ ____ ____.

The train ride gave me a fr____ ____ ____ ____.

Vowel sound: oa, ow, oe

Listen to the sound of **oa** in b**oa**t.

Listen to the same sound of **ow** in yell**ow**.

Listen to the same sound of **oe** in t**oe**.

1 Use these words and the picture clues to complete the word puzzle below.

> sparrow   coat   arrow   moat   elbow   toast   snowman   coast

1

2

3

4

5

6

7

8

Vowel sound: oo, ew, ue

Listen to the sound of **oo** in b**oo**t.

Listen to the sound of **ew** in n**ew**.

Listen to the same sound of **ue** in bl**ue**.

1 Find and circle these words with **oo**, **ew** and **ue**.

argue	chew	cool	few	flew	glue
jewel	moon	rescue	soon	tissue	zoo

i f e w x p i z o o
y s s o o n c d w q
j p h r e s c u e a
m m w p b z g l u e
o c h e w t t p l k
m o o n g a r g u e
q l x g l f l e w r
j e w e l j s e m f
t i s s u e p o h l
a a y c o o l f m s

2 Write a rhyming word in each space.

moon _____

zoo _____

Spelling pattern: ar

Listen to the sound of **ar** in sc**ar**f.

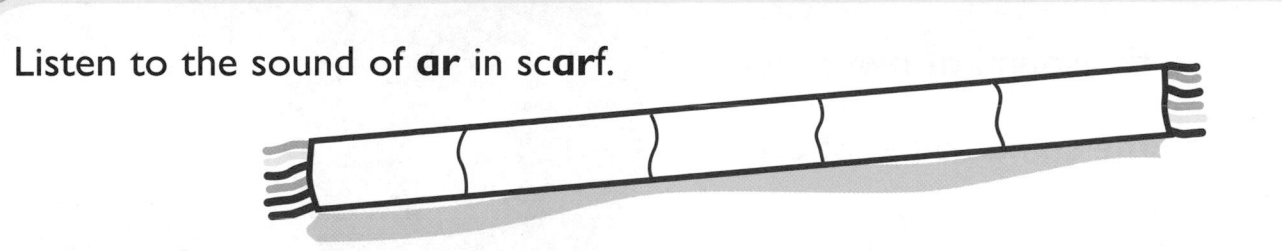

1 Write the letters below in the **ar** words on the scarf.

> p   ch   m   g   y

far_____   shar_____   part_____   mar_____   _____arden

2 Use the letters below to write rhyming words inside the shark and the star.

> c   p   j   d   m   f

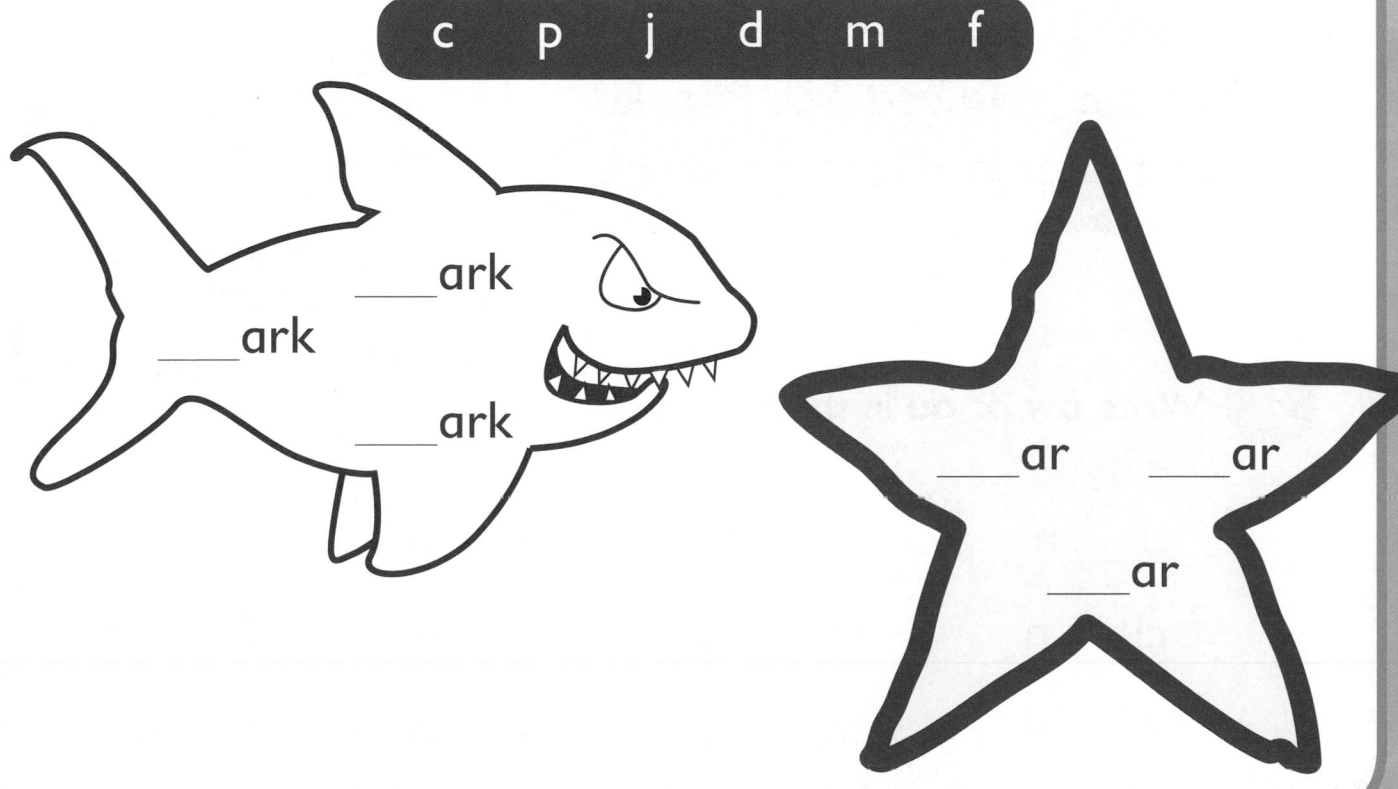

_____ark

_____ark

_____ark

_____ar   _____ar

_____ar

Spelling patterns: ow, ou

Listen to the sound of **ow** in **ow**l.

Listen to the same sound of **ou** in m**ou**se.

1   Read the rhyme aloud. Underline ten **ow** and **ou** words.

"Watch out!" called a cat
To a mouse by a tree,
"There's an owl on the prowl.
Why not hang out with me?"

So the mouse jumped down
From his hiding place.
The cat pounced and Mouse
Disappeared without a trace.

What did the owl say to his friend as he flew away?

"Owl be seeing you later!"

2   Write **ow** or **ou** in these words.

d___n	f___nd	br___n	h___se
cl___n	sh___er	c___nt	fl___er
v___el	m___th	s___nd	t___n

Spelling patterns: air, are, ear, ere

These rhyming words all share the same sound but have a different spelling pattern.

chair   spare   bear   there

1 Write these words in the correct column.

wear   there   repair   pear   stair   scare   where   spare

air	are	ear	ere

Some words sound the same but are spelt differently.

Where is my hat?

I want to **wear** it to the match.

Why did the doll blush?

Because she saw the teddy bear!

2 Circle the correct word to label each picture.

pear pair

hair hare

stair stare

bear bare

Spelling patterns: or, oor, aw, au, ore

These words all share the same sound but have a different spelling pattern.

for   door   paw   naughty   more

1 Write **or** in these words.

t____ch   f____k

st____y   st____m   st____k

2 Say these words out loud. Circle the odd one out.

lawn   dawn   thorn

down   corn   yawn

3 Join up the rhyming words.

floor   crawl   sport   caught   draw

short   snore   taught   law   shawl

Spelling patterns: er, ir, ur

These words all share the same sound but have a different spelling pattern.

tiger

bird

turtle

1 Label the pictures. Then write the words in the table. Add one more word of your own to each column.

sh_____

P_____

m_____

d_____

13

th_____

t_____

er	ir	ur

Encourage your child to think of words that contain the 'er' sound. Write them down and ask your child to count a total for each of the spelling patterns. They should notice that 'er' and 'ir' are the most common spelling pattern; 'ur' is much less common. Point out that 'er' is often found at the end of words; it is often used as a suffix (see pages 25 and 29).

Spelling patterns: wh, ph

Listen to the sound of **wh** in **wh**ale.

Listen to the sound of **ph** in ele**ph**ant.

1 These labels are spelt wrongly. Write the correct word.

dolfin ✗

weel ✗

fone ✗

_____   _____   _____

2 Join each question to the correct answer.

Why might you use a camera?   The **wh**ale

What do we call the letters a to z?   A s**ph**ere

Which sea animal is the largest?   To take a **ph**oto

What shape is round like a ball?   **Wh**ite

What colour is snow?   The al**ph**abet

Word endings: ing, ed, er

Adding **ing**, **ed** or **er** to a word changes its meaning.

paint → painting → painted → painter

1 Add **ing**, **ed** and **er** to each of these words

	+ing	+ed	+er
jump	_____	_____	_____
cook	_____	_____	_____
play	_____	_____	_____
buzz	_____	_____	

2 Write **three** things you like doing that end with **ing**.

painting   sticking   eating   jumping   singing

shouting   talking   playing   cooking

I like _____, _____

and _____.

Spelling patterns: ear, ea

Listen to the sound of **ear** in h**ear**.

1 Use the letters below to make words that rhyme with **ear**.

y
d
n
f
sp
r
cl
app

_____   _____

_____   _____

_____   _____

_____   _____

Listen to the sound of **ea** in h**ea**vy.

2 Join each word to a matching picture.

head

weather

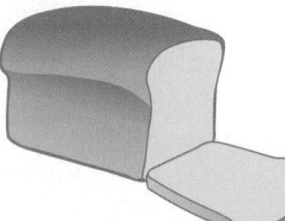

breakfast

bread

Compound words

A **compound** word is a word made up of two other words.

news + paper = newspaper

1 Join up the words to make new words. Write the new words.

water   cup   __waterfall__

tooth   house   _____

light   fall   _____

egg   day   _____

birth   brush   _____

2 Write the missing compound word in each joke.

> jellyfish   honeycomb   football   sunglasses

Why did the teacher wear _____?
Because her class was so bright!

Why did the _____ player wear a bib?
Because he was always dribbling!

What do _____ say at the start of a race?
Get set!

Why did the bee have sticky hair?
Because of his _____!

Prefix: un

We can add **un** in front of some words to change their meaning and make **opposite** words.

tidy

untidy

1 Use the prefix **un** to write a word that is opposite in meaning.

pack   <u>   unpack   </u>

well   _____

lucky   _____

locked   _____

kind   _____

fair   _____

true   _____

happy   _____

Adding er and est

Adding **er** or **est** to a word changes its meaning.

slow   slower   slowest

1 Add **er** and **est** to each of these words.

	+er	+est
near	nearer	nearest
loud		
soft		
old		
strong		
quick		
bright		
clever		

Spelling tips

Silly sentences can help you remember how to spell a word.

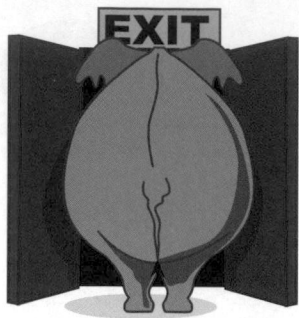

big elephants can't always use small exits ➔ because

gentle elephants never tackle little elephants ➔ gentle

1 Finish these silly sentences to help you remember how to spell **people** and **beauty**.

pink   big

elephants   elephants

o_____   a_____

p_____   u_____

l_____   t_____

e_____   y_____

Look for words inside words.

I like **ice** in my ju**ice**.

2 Underline a smaller word inside each of these words.

monkey   when   garage   chocolate

danger   brilliant   cupboard   comfortable

3 Hide each of these words inside a larger word.

put <u>computer</u>   elf _____   pin _____

owl _____   ear _____   itch _____

Watch out for silent letters.

com**b**

4 Circle the silent letter inside each of these words.

thumb   knee   write   honest

knit   castle   autumn   knight

Answers

Short vowels

Page 4

1. jam, pen, bun, zip
   bed, bag, wig, dog

2. cat – cut, leg – log

Syllables

Page 5

1. bat (1), carrot (2), frog (1)
   caravan (3), elephant (3), tiger (2)
   computer (3), snake (1), rainbow (2)

Long vowels with e

Page 6

1. cube, note, kite, plane

Page 7

2.

cake	make
rake	shake

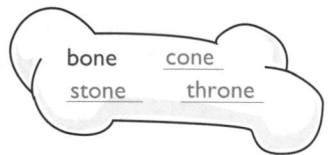

bone	cone
stone	throne

3. face, bike, rose, five, mole, dice

Spelling patterns: sh, ch, th

Page 8

1.

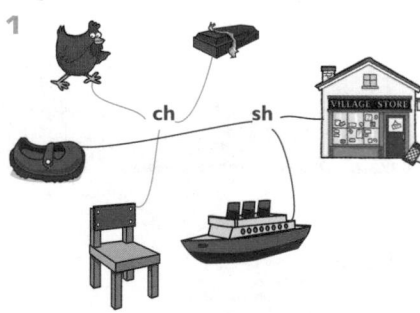

2. fish, beach, tooth, brush
   rush, moth, finish, lunch

Spelling pattern: tch

Page 9

1. match, catch, fetch, kitchen, notch,
   hutch, patch
   Other answers are possible.

Word ending: ck

Page 10

1. A mouse ran up the clock.
   The clock struck one,
   A mouse chewed a hole in my sock.
   My toe stuck out,

2. brick – sick, black – sack,
   check – peck, lock – sock,
   duck – truck

Spelling patterns: k, nk

Page 11

1. spooky, kid, ketchup, kennel, king,
   risky

2. think, link, stink, shrink, blink
   bank, junk, tank, trunk

Word endings: ff, ll, ss, zz

Page 12

1. Jill, hill
   princess, kiss
   huff, puff

More than one

Page 13

1. socks, bananas, sweets,
   dishes, boxes, monsters,
   sandwiches, spiders, octopuses

Vowel sound: ee, ea, ie, y

Page 14

1. Possible answers are:

bee
tree
sweet
three

2. fence, left

3. Child to read out words.

Vowel sound: ai, ay

Page 15

1.

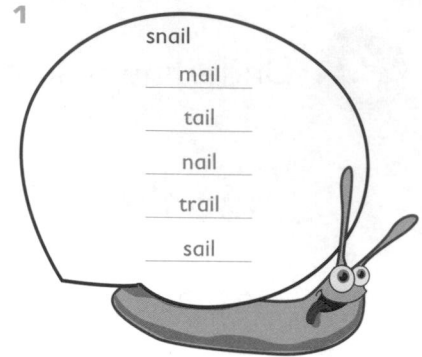

snail
mail
tail
nail
trail
sail

2. tray, train, today
   away, afraid, say
   clay, stay, paint

Vowel sound: ie, y, igh

Page 16

1. fly, cry, tie
   fry, pie, spy
   try, why, lie

2. night, slight
   flight, bright
   light, might
   right, sight

3. tight, fright

Vowel sound: oa, ow, oe

Page 17

1.

```
        ¹e          ²m
         l           o
         b           a
       ³t  o  a  ⁴s  t
         w           p
                     a
              ⁵c     r
     ⁶a  r  r  o  w  r
                     o
              a
           ⁷s  n  o  w  m  a  n
     ⁸c  o  a  t
```